WILD ANIMALS

BLACK MAMBAS

BY DALTON RAINS

WWW.APEXEDITIONS.COM

Copyright © 2026 by Apex Editions, Mendota Heights, MN 55120. All rights reserved. No part of this book may be reproduced or utilized in any form or by any means without written permission from the publisher.

Apex is distributed by North Star Editions:
sales@northstareditions.com | 888-417-0195

Produced for Apex by Red Line Editorial.

Photographs ©: Shutterstock Images, cover, 1, 4–5, 6, 7, 8, 9, 10–11, 12–13, 14, 15, 16–17, 18, 19, 20, 21, 22–23, 24, 25, 26–27, 29

Library of Congress Control Number: 2024952628

ISBN
979-8-89250-545-1 (hardcover)
979-8-89250-581-9 (paperback)
979-8-89250-649-6 (ebook pdf)
979-8-89250-617-5 (hosted ebook)

Printed in the United States of America
Mankato, MN
082025

NOTE TO PARENTS AND EDUCATORS

Apex books are designed to build literacy skills in striving readers. Exciting, high-interest content attracts and holds readers' attention. The text is carefully leveled to allow students to achieve success quickly. Additional features, such as bolded glossary words for difficult terms, help build comprehension.

TABLE OF CONTENTS

CHAPTER 1
FIGHTING BACK 4

CHAPTER 2
MASSIVE MAMBAS 10

CHAPTER 3
HIDING AND HUNTING 16

CHAPTER 4
LIFE CYCLE 22

COMPREHENSION QUESTIONS • 28
GLOSSARY • 30
TO LEARN MORE • 31
ABOUT THE AUTHOR • 31
INDEX • 32

CHAPTER 1

FIGHTING BACK

A black mamba rests on a rock. Suddenly, a lion appears. The snake tries to slither away. But it is cornered.

Black mambas often rest in sunny spots to warm up.

Black mambas may try to scare off attackers when cornered.

The mamba raises its head above the ground. It spreads flaps on its neck and opens its mouth. Then the snake lets out a loud hiss.

FAST FACT
A mamba's fangs fold out when its mouth opens.

A black mamba's fangs are only about 0.26 inches (0.65 cm) long.

DEADLY SNAKE

A black mamba has powerful **venom**. The venom attacks an animal's **nerves** and heart. It may **paralyze** the animal. The animal's heart may stop beating.

A black mamba's venom can kill an animal in minutes.

Antivenom can treat snakebites. To make this medicine, scientists milk venom out of snakes' fangs.

The lion pounces on the mamba. But the snake strikes back. Its fangs sink into the lion's neck. The lion yelps and jumps back in pain. The snake gets away to safety.

CHAPTER 2

MASSIVE MAMBAS

Black mambas are large snakes. Most adults are about 8 feet (2.4 m) long. But some grow up to 14 feet (4.3 m).

An adult black mamba weighs about 3.5 pounds (1.6 kg).

Black mambas are not actually black. Their scales can be brown, green, or gray. These colors help the snakes hide among plants and rocks.

BEHIND THE NAME

A black mamba opens its mouth when in danger. The inside of the snake's mouth is dark. That's what the black mamba is named after.

◀ The dark color of a black mamba's mouth acts as a warning to other animals.

A black mamba uses its sense of smell when hunting. The snake flicks out its tongue to bring in air. Then it uses an **organ** in its mouth to smell.

Black mambas have excellent eyesight. It helps the snakes sense movement.

A black mamba's scales work like hooks. They grip the ground and help the snake move.

FAST FACT

Black mambas can slither more than 12 miles per hour (19 km/h).

CHAPTER 3

Hiding and Hunting

Black mambas live in southern and eastern Africa. They are the longest venomous snakes on the **continent**.

The black mamba is one of four types of mamba. Each kind lives in Africa.

Black mambas travel on the ground most of the time. But they sometimes move through trees.

Many black mambas live in **savannas** or hilly areas. Others live in forests. Mambas tend to stay near rocks or fallen trees. The snakes use these objects for cover.

OUT OF SIGHT

Black mambas are mostly shy. They attack only when there is no way to escape a **threat**. So, the snakes often keep out of sight. Mambas sometimes sleep in empty termite mounds or animal **burrows**.

Black mambas may use the same sleeping hole or tree for years.

Adult black mambas eat only once or twice a week.

Mambas leave their hiding spots to hunt. They often attack small animals. After biting, a mamba waits until its prey stops moving. Then the snake swallows the animal.

FAST FACT

Just two drops of black mamba venom can kill most humans.

A black mamba's mouth can open very wide. That lets the snake swallow animals whole.

CHAPTER 4

LIFE CYCLE

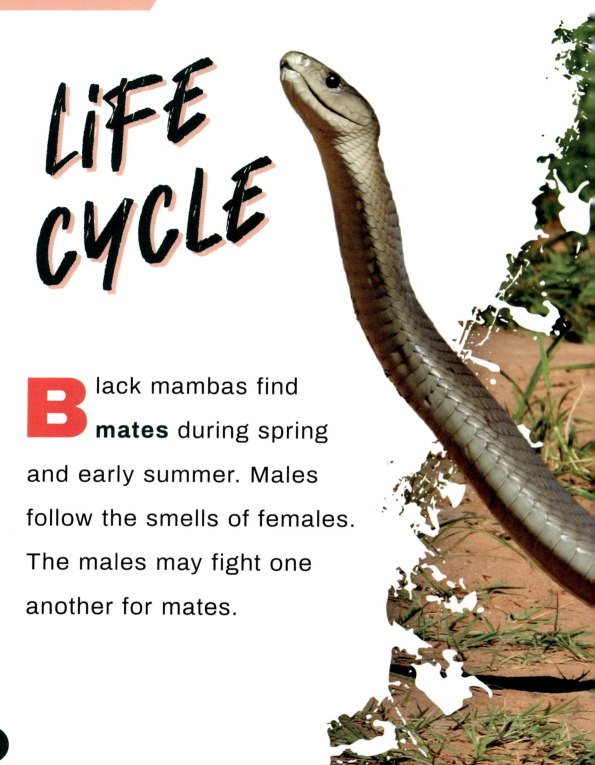

Black mambas find **mates** during spring and early summer. Males follow the smells of females. The males may fight one another for mates.

Black mambas may travel long distances to find mates.

Newly hatched black mambas are about 20 inches (50 cm) long.

A black mamba lays 6 to 20 eggs in a hidden place. Then, the mother leaves. The eggs hatch after two to three months.

FACING DANGER

Black mambas don't have many predators. But mongooses and honey badgers sometimes hunt the snakes. A black mamba's venom is not as harmful to those animals.

When attacked, black mambas strike back. The snakes use lots of venom to keep animals away.

Young mambas must hunt and fight for themselves right away. The snakes grow quickly. Within a year, they are more than 6 feet (1.8 m) long.

FAST FACT
Young mambas have only a few drops of venom in each fang. Older snakes have 12 to 20 drops.

Black mambas can live 10 years or more.

COMPREHENSION QUESTIONS

Write your answers on a separate piece of paper.

1. Write a few sentences explaining the main ideas of Chapter 3.

2. Which feature of black mambas do you find most interesting? Why?

3. How long are most adult black mambas?
    - **A.** 6 feet (1.8 m)
    - **B.** 8 feet (2.4 m)
    - **C.** 14 feet (4.3 m)

4. Which area would a black mamba most likely avoid?
    - **A.** a hilly area with lots of rocks
    - **B.** a desert with lots of open space
    - **C.** a grassy area with lots of fallen trees

5. What does **pounces** mean in this book?

*The lion **pounces** on the mamba. But the snake strikes back. Its fangs sink into the lion's neck.*

    A. stays still
    B. runs away from something
    C. jumps toward something

6. What does **predators** mean in this book?

*Black mambas don't have many **predators**. But mongooses and honey badgers sometimes hunt the snakes.*

    A. animals that kill and eat other animals
    B. animals that eat only plants
    C. animals that rarely eat

Answer key on page 32.

GLOSSARY

burrows
Tunnels or holes that animals use as homes.

continent
One of the seven large pieces of land on Earth.

mates
Animals that come together to have babies.

nerves
Long, thin fibers that carry information between the brain and other parts of the body.

organ
A part of the body that has a specific job.

paralyze
To make something unable to move.

savannas
Flat, grassy areas with few or no trees.

threat
Something that is likely to cause danger or harm.

venom
A poison made by an animal and used to bite or sting prey.

TO LEARN MORE

BOOKS

Jaycox, Jaclyn. *Mambas*. Capstone Publishing, 2021.

Levy, Janey. *Black Mamba vs. Blue-Ringed Octopus.* Gareth Stevens Publishing, 2022.

Sommer, Nathan. *Black Mamba vs. Caracal*. Bellwether Media, 2024.

ONLINE RESOURCES

Visit **www.apexeditions.com** to find links and resources related to this title.

ABOUT THE AUTHOR

Dalton Rains is an author and editor from Saint Paul, Minnesota. He enjoys living far away from black mambas.

INDEX

A
Africa, 16

B
burrows, 19

C
continent, 16

E
eggs, 24

F
fangs, 7, 9, 27
flaps, 6

H
hunting, 14, 20, 25–26

N
nerves, 8

O
organ, 14

P
paralyzing, 8
predators, 25

S
savannas, 18
scales, 13

T
threat, 19

V
venom, 8, 16, 21, 25, 27

ANSWER KEY:
1. Answers will vary; 2. Answers will vary; 3. B; 4. B; 5. C; 6. A